Rochester History

SPRING 2023

Rochester History

A publication of the Rochester Public Library
in partnership with Rochester Institute of Technology

Volume 80, Issue 2

Contents

DIRECTOR'S CORNER

In this edition of the *Rochester History* journal, Jennifer M. Lloyd examines the life and contributions of Martha Taylor Howard, acknowledging her as the woman who helped secure Susan B. Anthony's legacy and home in Rochester, New York. An enthusiastic participant in the women's club movement in the early to mid-twentieth century, Howard used every connection she had to raise funds, buy Anthony's house, and renovate it into a piece of living history reminding visitors of the tremendous legacy Anthony created. Indeed, Howard replicated the spirit of Anthony's own suffrage work, showing remarkable perseverance in the face of dismissiveness, ridicule, and failure. The author paints Howard as a clever and persistent woman unwilling to accept anything less than the success of her vision. I was struck by a quote very early in the article in which Howard acknowledges her own privilege and the responsibility that accompanies it: "Having lineage entails a responsibility. If you have noteworthy ancestors you should do something about it." Howard clearly felt a responsibility for securing the legacy of Susan B. Anthony, and in the twenty-first century, Rochester is better for her efforts. ■

Patty Uttaro
Director, Rochester Public Library

LETTER FROM THE EDITORS

Dear reader,

We are delighted to introduce you to a reimagined and expanded *Rochester History* journal. *Rochester History* was established in 1939 by then-Assistant Rochester City Historian Blake McKelvey. McKelvey was a nationally renowned scholar who was, and still is, recognized as one of the pioneers of the then-new field of urban history. His work, and the journal he founded, also helped to establish local history as a valued field of study. Building upon the foundation McKelvey laid, subsequent city historians and journal editors have carried on his mission of increasing knowledge of and interest in local history and culture and of placing local issues into national or global contexts. Today, *Rochester History* is widely recognized as a premier source of scholarship on the history of Greater Rochester and the Genesee Valley.

Now, we are embarking on a path that will ensure that this legacy not only continues but grows. The Rochester Public Library, which has published the journal since 1939, has signed an agreement with Rochester Institute of Technology's Department of History and RIT Press to jointly produce this and future issues of the journal. The partnership will allow us to add content and expand the journal's reach and impact by taking advantage of new technologies. In this issue, the first to be produced under this partnership, we invite readers to reconsider the things we think we know about our shared past.

Our feature article, "Martha Taylor Howard and the Campaign to Preserve the Susan B. Anthony House," explores how what is today the National Susan B. Anthony Museum & House came into existence and asks us to reflect on the role of one oft-forgotten local woman played in preserving Anthony's home. One particularly visible part of our new partnership—and one that long-time readers will immediately notice—is the addition of new features, including reviews of books, exhibits, films, and other sources of historical information, such as those found in this inaugural issue. You will see more new features unveiled in future issues. Here, you will find Michael Brown's review of Laura Warren Hill's book *Strike the Hammer: The Black Freedom Struggle in Rochester, New York, 1940–1970*, which reconsiders the history of race in Rochester, asking us to look again at both the roots and the aftermath of the racial uprising in Rochester in 1964. Our editorial team was fortunate to be able to interview Hill about her work, and you will find a lightly edited version of that conversation in this issue.

Also in this issue, Shanleigh Corrallo explores the public memory of the Attica

Prison Rebellion of 1971 in the wake of its recent fiftieth anniversary. She reviews *Attica*, a 2021 documentary film, as well as the exhibit *Open Wounds: The 50-Year Legacy of the Attica Prison Uprising*, a traveling exhibit curated by staff at the New York State Museum. In Rochester, the state exhibit was supplemented with additional content—curated by the city historian, a local journalist, and a documentary filmmaker—that explores the uprising's *Local Connections*. As Corrallo points out, the anniversary of the prison uprising arrived in the wake of protests over the deaths of George Floyd and Daniel Prude while in police custody in 2020; then, as now, issues of mass incarceration, criminal justice reform, and police brutality sparked critical community conversations.

We hope all of the offerings in this inaugural issue will encourage readers to reflect on local history and to reconsider the ways in which the legacy of our shared past continues to inform our lives in Rochester today. Welcome and enjoy! ■

Christine L. Ridarsky & Rebecca Edwards
Editors

Martha Taylor Howard and the Campaign to Preserve the Susan B. Anthony House

by Jennifer M. Lloyd

Martha Taylor Howard was already in her mid-sixties when she moved to Rochester, New York, in 1939. A woman of moderate means with very few local ties, Howard quickly formed alliances and friendships through membership in local women's clubs, where her boundless energy, enthusiasm, and persistence was directed at promoting the welfare of women and girls. But few could have predicted the lasting effect that Howard's presence would have on the community. In addition to her service to women and girls, Howard was the prime mover in the acquisition and renovation of what is now one of the city's best-known landmarks, the Susan B. Anthony House. Yet Howard is hardly remembered today.

Martha Taylor Howard was born in 1875 on Old Oaken Bucket Farm in Westford, Massachusetts, a small manufacturing town (population 1,448 in 1880) about 36 miles from Boston. Her family, descendants of the influential Adams family that produced two US presidents, traced its ancestry back to the American Revolution. Her father, Samuel Law Taylor, was a respected member of the community, a successful farmer, a member of the Grange (a national farmers' association), and a writer of columns for the local weekly newsletter.[1] Her mother, Alta Schellinger Taylor, of Swedish descent, had worked in the nearby Lowell cotton mills, to which the owners recruited girls from local farms,

Jennifer M. Lloyd is a retired associate professor in history at SUNY Brockport. She is a graduate of Cambridge University (UK) and received her PhD from the University of Rochester. She is the author of *Women and the Shaping of British Methodism* and several scholarly articles on women's history. She volunteers in the Susan B. Anthony House archives.

Martha Taylor Howard and her family, ca. 1896. From left to right: Mary Schellinger, (aunt), Alta Schellinger Taylor (mother), Ester Taylor (sister), Samuel Law Taylor (father), Martha Taylor Howard. Below: John Taylor (brother), unknown. *Photograph courtesy of James Howard.*

providing them with safe living conditions, higher-than-normal wages for the textile industry, and educational opportunities. Following her marriage, Alta Taylor was one of the first women elected to a school board after Massachusetts recognized, in 1879, women's right to vote in school board elections.[2] Thus, Howard grew up in a family that was conscious of its role in the nation's history and its position in the local community, one which valued women's education. Her obituary reported, "Patriotic to the core, Mrs. Howard felt a deep responsibility to preserve the ideals upon which this country was founded."[3] She herself had once stated, "Having lineage entails a responsibility. If you have noteworthy ancestors you should do something about it."[4]

The family's comfortable circumstances and her mother's belief in education for girls ensured that Howard attended the local Westford Academy, a private coeducational school with a demanding curriculum in both the classics and science. She was a member of the last class to graduate in the old building that the school was rapidly outgrowing.[5] Following her commencement in 1896, Howard enrolled in the independent private women's college, Mount Holyoke, becoming one of the 85,000 college women who made up just under 36 percent of the total US undergraduate population.[6] Mount Holyoke was a pioneer in women's education, the first of the Seven Sisters founded to provide female students with an Ivy League-quality curriculum while placing a strong emphasis on women's rights.[7] The suffragist Lucy Stone was an alumnus. Howard was admitted to the literary concentration and during her undergraduate years was class secretary and a yearbook editor, as well as a member of the YWCA, the athletic association, and the executive committee of the debating society.[8] She graduated in 1899 but stayed on to complete a master of arts in 1901.[9]

Her advanced education in a prestigious women's college made Howard part of the cohort known as the "New Women," a phrase first used in the 1890s and later defined by historian Jean Matthews as "young, well educated, . . . independent of spirit, highly competent, and physically strong and fearless."[10] She was part of a second generation of college-educated women's rights activists that included Carrie Chapman Catt and Harriot Stanton Blatch. Like many of her peers, upon graduation Howard sought employment rather than marriage, opting to go into education. She taught elementary school for a year before taking a position teaching psychology at Western College in Ohio, an offshoot of Mount Holyoke, although her qualification in psychology was owing to a single undergraduate course in the discipline, and her obituary stated she taught English.[11] According to the weekly *Westford Wardsman,* Howard stayed in Ohio for some years.[12] Her younger sister's marriage in 1905 likely brought her back to Westford.[13] From there she seems to have drifted a little. In 1908, she went with other Westford residents on a three-month tour of Great Britain, with a side trip to France. Much later, when entertaining the British Consul in Western New York, she remembered the many times they were served tea and "thought it so romantic. So much time and formality was put into the serving. In Scotland high tea included rabbit pie."[14]

Martha Taylor Howard donning her graduation robe following the completion of her master's degree in 1901. *Photograph courtesy of James Howard.*

On her return from Europe, she spent more than a year living with her cousin Gilbert Schellinger and his wife in Franklin, New Jersey, working as a teacher.

Adjacent to Franklin was Bound Brook, where a stock trader, George Howard, lived with his parents, farmers with land in the Catskills and New Jersey and a presence in the wool trade.[15] George was an independent dealer in the New York curb exchange, described in an article in *Munsey's Magazine* as "a roaring, swirling whirlpool" of largely unregulated trading.[16] Somehow the two thirty-somethings met and fell in love. Howard returned to Westford in 1909 to prepare for her wedding.[17] The 1910 census listed her as a schoolteacher, unemployed for 30 weeks.[18]

Marriage and Motherhood

Martha Taylor and George Howard married on June 25, 1910, at the Taylor family home in Westford. She was 34; he, 37. It was a quiet wedding, in contrast to the much larger affair held earlier for Martha's sister. The rooms were decorated "with ferns, June roses and beautiful pink laurel" from the woods, and a Congregational minister officiated. They had no formal honeymoon but spent the month of July in Westford before leaving for New Jersey on a boat from Boston Harbor.[19]

Martha Taylor and George Howard on their wedding day, June 25, 1910. *Photograph courtesy of James Howard.*

The Howards resided in Bound Brook for twenty years. According to the 1915 New Jersey census, they were living with George's family in a household with nine people.[20] Their son George Taylor Howard was born in 1914 in Westford, where Howard had traveled for the birth. In April 1918, their second son, Lawrence Salisbury, was christened, also in Westford.[21] Eight years later, tragedy struck the family when Lawrence died, likely of scarlet fever. Howard left no record of her grief, and there is no mention of Lawrence in her surviving papers—her silence may be a measure of her and George's immense loss, compounded by her mother's death in 1922.[22]

Little is known about George and Martha's relationship, but an incident Howard recalled in 1960, probably referring to the first time she voted after the Nineteenth Amendment was ratified, suggests a little about George's character. She noted that she was a "rock-ribbed" Republican and he a Democrat, but claimed: "He did not want me to change and I never tried to get him to change his party. We never had any words about politics. I voted first and then when we had finished voting, he said to me 'I voted Republican for the first time. I didn't want my vote to nullify yours.'"[23] Howard's Republicanism was of the type described by Catherine Rymph as tending to "view politics as an act of love or of civic duty."[24] She came from a solid Massachusetts Republican family and never questioned her allegiance. Active in local politics after 1920, she organized a New Jersey chapter of the League of Women Voters.[25]

George's fortunes fluctuated during this time, and on one occasion George Jr. was sent to live with relatives.[26] In the 1920s, the couple moved to 101 W. 55th Street in New York City. By 1930, George Jr. was away at Deerfield Academy in Massachusetts, and Martha Howard was listed in the census as a housewife.[27] As an independent trader, George must have been badly hit by the 1929 Crash, and 1929–30 was likely the year he stopped trading independently and began working as a "customers' man" (i.e., representative) for the brokerage firm Bouvier & Co., founded by Jacqueline Kennedy Onassis's grandfather. George's obituary described him as "of great business acumen and held in great respect . . . because of his integrity, loyalty and ability."[28] But just as the family had attained some financial stability, disaster struck again. In 1931, George contracted an undiagnosed disease and died in 1933, after twenty-three years of marriage.[29] Howard was in her early fifties. Years later she occasionally mentioned the effects of George's death. In a letter of condolence to another woman, she wrote, "I try to live as seeing him who is invisible—and I try to do what he would expect me to do."[30] She wrote to the widow of Willard Leuscher, longtime treasurer of the Susan B. Anthony Foundation: "When my husband passed on I was comforted by the thought that I could get along better alone, than he could if I had gone first."[31] In another letter penned more than twenty-five years after George's death, she wrote, "I have tried to live as he would wish me to live and not sadden others."[32]

George's death left Howard without a steady income. George Jr. was an undergraduate at Amherst, and she was alone.[33] Courageously, she decided to seek work as a freelance journalist. In a draft of a letter, she described "wonderful" and "excellent" training from women journalists at the *Tribune* and *New York Times*. She received a blue ribbon for editorial excellence, had several articles printed in both papers and in the *New York Sun*, and was the press representative for several groups in the city for ten years. She maintained her membership in the Women's Press Club of New York City until her death and was often asked to "say something" when she visited from Rochester.[34]

An important aspect of Howard's life that provided some solace was her membership in women's clubs. From the 1860s onward, thousands of middle-class women, mostly married housewives, joined clubs that stressed personal growth and intellectual improvement, giving them experience in public speaking and organizing, and, by the 1920s, an understanding that women could and should participate as public citizens.[35] By 1910, the General Federation of Women's Clubs represented nearly a million members. Historian Nancy Cott has suggested that "it is highly probable that the greatest extent of associational activity in the whole history of American women took place in the era between the two world wars."[36] Howard was typical of women of her generation, for whom club membership provided both a social life and an outlet for activism. Her pride in her heritage meant that her greatest allegiances were to the Daughters of the American Revolution (DAR), a national organization that doubled in size between 1910 and 1932, and the National Society of New England Women, first organized in 1895—around the time she graduated from high school.[37] She also served as president of the New England Women's New York City colony. After George's death, she became radio award chair for the National Federation of Press Women.[38] Her club work gave her confidence, community, and valuable contacts, as she was about to find out.

Move to Rochester

In 1939, after graduating from Amherst College and Harvard Business School with an engineering degree, George Jr. found employment at the Eastman Kodak Co.[39] Howard decided to move to Rochester with him. He had been dating a woman his mother deemed unsuitable, and, as her granddaughter later surmised, Howard wanted to keep an eye on whomever he married.[40] She and George Jr. rented a house at 429 Seneca Parkway, within walking distance of Kodak, for $45 a month.[41] Howard arrived in Rochester in her mid-sixties after a busy life in New York City. She had no obvious role except as mother of a grown son, but, as a consummate clubwoman, she had contacts. The previous year she had visited the city for a luncheon organized by the Rochester chapter of the Society of New England Women, and shortly after she arrived in October 1939, she gave a reception for three national officers of the organization.[42] She transferred her membership in the Daughters of the American Revolution from New Jersey to Rochester, where she joined its committees for approved schools, conservation, and publicity and became a Regent. Her greatest allegiance remained to those two organizations, in which she held national office and attended nationwide meetings.[43] They encouraged her ardent patriotism and her interest in both history and women's issues. As she put it, "I have a deep seated feeling that we should maintain stoutly the principles upon which this country was founded—because those principles were RIGHT and so are eternal, for right is eternal and not temporary."[44]

These were not her only interests. Howard joined the Rundel chapter of the Delphian Society, an organization established to encourage women's education through reading, and served as a seminar discussant on creative thinking and became the society's publicity person.[45] Her obituary lists fifteen clubs in which she held office, while her activity in many others, such as the local Friends of Children and the Council of American Youth Hostels, can be tracked through the pages of the *Democrat & Chronicle* newspaper. She acted as press officer and/or radio officer for several of these organizations, drawing on the expertise she developed during her time in New York City. A local reporter maintained that Howard held, "probably an all-time record as a press chairman."[46] Judy Bennett, a journalist for the *Democrat & Chronicle,* described her as a "plump, little rosy-cheeked woman with the wisps of white hair tucked into a flower-trimmed hat," who was nonetheless a "darned good news source," always accurate, concise, and relevant.[47]

Martha Howard's and George Jr. Howard's Tudor-style residence at 429 Seneca Parkway in Rochester's Maplewood neighborhood, 2021. *Photograph courtesy of Jennifer M. Lloyd.*

In Rochester, Howard became a committed Christian Scientist. She had been raised a Congregationalist (although her father preferred the Unitarian church and sang in its choir) and was married by a Congregational minister.[48] The local Westford newsletter described her as "so helpful a member" of the church there.[49] But her closest place of worship in Rochester was the Second Church of Christ Scientist (now Emmanuel Temple) at the end of Seneca Parkway, and its proximity to her home may have tempted her to explore the services. Christian Science, founded by Mary Baker Eddy, promised health and the control of one's life through the power of thought and was particularly attractive to women.[50] Howard subscribed and occasionally contributed to the *Christian Science Monitor* and claimed sisterhood with Christian Science correspondents, notably Alma Lutz, Susan B. Anthony's biographer, who became a good friend. Howard noted that she had "accomplished all that I have

. . . according to Christian Science principles."[51] Her granddaughter remembers seeing the mosaics during services at the First Church of Christian Science, now the Lyric Theatre.[52]

The Susan B. Anthony House

Howard's interest in Susan B. Anthony began after she moved to Rochester. In 1942, she was elected president of the Rochester Federation of Women's Clubs, an organization Anthony had founded. Her election was surprising, since she had been in Rochester only three years and had attended meetings only as a club representative and was not on the Executive Board. The board minutes for April 1942 noted that there were no nominations for president, and that "this was discussed and names submitted." Howard's energy, experience, and intelligence would have been obvious, and hers must have been one of the names listed, since by July she was chairing meetings as president.[53] She later noted that her interest in Anthony began when she was "made President of the Federation of Women's Clubs and found that Susan B. Anthony had organized it in 1898 and that Miss Anthony had also been the first to propose that women be represented on the school board," something that would have resonated with her because of her mother.[54] Anthony was, in Howard's view, a determined and patriotic woman who had been overlooked. In 1945, she told a *Democrat & Chronicle* reporter that after her move to Rochester she "started asking influential Rochesterials [*sic*] why something was not done about memorializing Miss Anthony, perhaps the city's most outstanding woman citizen of its history, by taking over and maintaining her old house as a public shrine." In 1957, another reporter quoted her as saying, "When I came to Rochester and became president of the group whom [*sic*] Susan B. Anthony had founded and learned that people here didn't even know where her home was I knew something should be done."[55]

In the years since the Nineteenth Amendment was ratified, public interest in Susan B. Anthony had waned. In 1925, social reformer and Rochesterian Helen Barrett Montgomery had urged the purchase of the Anthony house by local women's groups, but nothing had happened.[56] In 1929, below a headline that read, "Grave Forgotten by All but One, Susan Anthony's Birthday Passes," the *Democrat and Chronicle* reported that only the male founder of the Susan B. Anthony Little Girls Club had laid a wreath at Anthony's burial site. Admittedly, the February weather was bad.[57] Emma B. Sweet, secretary to Susan B. Anthony in her final years, kept Anthony's name alive in Rochester with birthday teas. The suffragist's great-niece, Susan B. Anthony II, while an undergraduate at the University of Rochester in the late 1930s, was asked by Sweet to wear her great-aunt's garnet silk dress at one of the events.[58]

Rose Arnold Powell, a member of the Minnesota Federation of Women's Clubs and an ardent Anthony promoter, wrote to Howard that the General Federation of Women's Clubs had failed to build a memorial to Anthony in Washington, D.C., in the 1920s: "I saw that a long campaign of education was necessary before women would be interested enough to support such an effort." She noted that before his death in 1941, sculptor Gutzon Borglum had agreed to carve Susan B. Anthony on Mount Rushmore, but "I couldn't rouse women in time to care enough about the honor to work for it wholeheartedly." Powell complained that women's organizations were "too individualistic to work together as a unit" and that "our women pioneers spent a lifetime begging, pleading, appealing to men, unable to command anything."[59] William B. Browne, the person responsible for the upkeep of the Susan B. Anthony birthplace in Adams, Massachusetts, wrote to Howard, "It is difficult here to get any appreciation of Miss Anthony in any way."[60]

Howard's first initiative was to remind the public of Susan B. Anthony's former presence in Rochester. On May 12, 1944, at the annual meeting of the Rochester Federation of Women's Clubs, with Howard presiding, the group passed a resolution "for the placing of a suitable wooden plaque at the house." Howard would be responsible for making it happen.[61] This proved difficult since wartime shortages had put wood in short supply, and they had to compromise on masonite.[62] They dedicated the marker in a brief ceremony on October 26, 1944, with Florence Mosher, another of Susan B. Anthony's great-nieces, present. After the proceedings, Howard and five other women stayed behind under the horse chestnut tree, talking about "Miss Anthony's courage, perseverance and devotion to a cause." The house owner, a widow who lived there with her son, invited one of them, Grace Schneider, inside, where she discovered in conversation that the owner wanted to sell the house, which was getting to be too much for them. Schneider came out, collected a dollar from each of the women, and presented it to Howard in a "lovely Roman striped silk container," telling her it was a down payment for the house purchase and that she should organize it. Howard later recalled, "It was a challenge/What should I do?—either I must give the money back or follow through and buy the house. In the face of all that Miss Anthony endured in her lifetime I knew that I could not be cowardly and return the money."[63] Here was a challenge worthy of her organizing skills and determination. She was nearly seventy years old.

Raising the Money

The Federation of Women's Clubs resolved to purchase the house on November 10, 1944, and agreed to incorporate The Susan B. Anthony Memorial, Inc.[64] They took out a six-month option to buy. The asking price was $8,500 (almost $144,500 in 2023).[65] The house was in good condition but required some repairs to the roof and gutters.[66] The Memorial needed to raise about $10,000 for the purchase, repairs, painting, and conversion of the house into what Howard called a "shrine."[67] She was aware that there was a precedent for a women's organization owning a national site. The Mount Vernon Ladies' Association owned and maintained George Washington's home in Virginia, partially funded by nationwide donations collected by state vice-regents. Edwine Danforth, a well-known Rochester hostess with a long history of community service, was a local vice-regent and may have suggested the idea to Howard.[68] However, the Mount Vernon Ladies had launched a national campaign to raise $200,000 to secure the estate, far more than the cost required for the Susan B. Anthony purchase. Howard needed a local approach.[69]

She knew of another precedent for a successful fundraising campaign, one run by the Christian Science Publishing Company. She decided to copy its method and went against her board's wishes, deciding not to have a "drive" to solicit money door-to-door.[70] Instead, "We would have no big social to start it off but just announce the project in the papers and let the public know of the opportunity and privilege that was theirs."[71] Several times she reiterated, "I did not ask people for money."[72] She wanted it to be a women's effort: "The idea came to me that we would make use of women as far as possible."[73] Not to have a drive may have been a wise decision, as there were already campaigns to sell War Bonds, with the Rochester Federation of Women's Clubs heavily involved, and the city was starting to raise funds for the Community War Memorial.[74] Although the Federation set up a fundraising group, Howard was personally responsible for most of the work, targeting individuals whom she believed were potential donors.[75] A visitor to the house described her methods: "In asking for donations, Mrs. Howard wrote very clever letters. She told what others had done, and then said, 'If you wish to consider a new kitchen sink (or whatever) your name will of course be placed nearby.'"[76] And the contributions came in, in small amounts from individuals and larger ones from local organizations and businesses such as McCurdy's, B. Forman, and the Rochester Business and Professional Women's Club.[77] On one day in May 1945, for example, the Memorial's Treasurer, Willard Leuscher, logged nine contributions, ranging from single dollars from individuals to $10.85 from West High School to McCurdy's $150 donation.[78]

Some potential major local donors disappointed. Maria Gannett, mother of newspaper magnate Frank E. Gannett, thought people should support "Aunt Susan's' active causes," meaning local and national organizations. Frank Gannett, however, contributed through the League of Women Voters, and was himself a strong supporter of Howard's efforts, giving the campaign free press coverage.[79] Eleanor Gleason, sister of the engineer Kate Gleason, declined to donate, thinking the asking price for the house was too high. Kodak also refused to contribute.[80] Raising money outside Rochester proved difficult. Howard reached out to surviving suffragists but was let down, noting in a 1946 letter: "I thought the project of buying the house would bring forth letters from people who worked with Miss Anthony or whose relatives did. But that has not been the case."[81]

Her major ally from the suffrage campaign was Carrie Chapman Catt, the leader of the National American Woman Suffrage Association (NAWSA) when the Nineteenth Amendment was passed, who took considerable interest in the project. Catt collected contributions from the NAWSA board, including $700 from the billionaire and major supporter of women's causes Katherine McCormick. Mrs. Robert Anderson, chair of the Susan B. Anthony Memorial Committee of the National Women's Party, sent $100.[82] Eleanor Roosevelt also sent a donation and wrote about the House in her newspaper column.[83] Yet Howard wrote to Catt, "I think I know how Miss Anthony felt when she did not get quick success. But she never let herself get discouraged I believe. So too, I feel we will in the end get the money—but I wanted it to come in quicker."[84] Nonetheless, the achievement was remarkable. By December 1945, they had raised enough money to make a payment of $5,000, take out a mortgage of $3,340, and receive the deed for the house. By the following December, they had paid off the mortgage and had about $1,500 in hand.[85] Catt sent the last $700 needed for the mortgage, the remaining balance in the million-dollar fund Mrs. Frank Leslie had left to her in 1914 to fund the suffrage campaign.[86]

Securing the house for posterity put Howard in touch with other women in what historian Leila Rupp described as "a loose network of women dedicated to winning recognition for the pioneers of the suffrage movement," notably the dedicated Anthony supporter Rose Arnold Powell of Minnesota, Christian Scientist and Anthony biographer Alma Lutz, and Carrie Chapman Catt.[87] Howard asked all of them for advice on several occasions. She never met either Powell or

Catt but had extensive correspondence with them, while Lutz became a valued friend. She also corresponded with Rochester native Florence Kitchelt, tireless promoter of the Equal Rights Amendment in Connecticut.[88]

Opening the House

The next hurdle for the house was to renovate and furnish the interior. Here, the Federation board and women in the Rochester community played a major role. First, the previous owners had to move, a difficult task given the post-war housing shortage, but the Federation was finally able to take possession in October 1946.[89] Then Howard, in consultation with the Foundation board, decided to ask local, state, and national bodies to fund the renovation of particular rooms. This proved to be much easier than trying to raise more money herself. The department store B. Forman, the Women's Alliance of the Unitarian Church, the State Department of the Women's Relief Corporation, some of Susan B. Anthony's relatives, the classroom teachers of Rochester, the Business and Professional Women of New York, the National Association of New England Women, the University of Rochester Women Alumnae, and the Board of the National Association for Woman Suffrage all came forward. Individuals and organizations also donated furniture, furnishings, books, letters, and other materials. Catt donated the desk on which she had drafted the Nineteenth Amendment, as well as her personal collection of more than 125 framed portraits of woman suffragists.[90]

The house's annual upkeep needed to be funded at an estimated cost of $1,000 a year. At first, Howard hoped that another organization would take it over, telling the Federation's committee, "After we purchase the Home . . . we will turn it over to the Rochester Museum. Mr. Parker [the museum head] says they will maintain it, paying all costs . . . We will be custodians. This can be worked out later to the satisfaction of everyone."[91] That plan fell through. She approached the New York State Historical Society, the Rochester Historical Society, the Landmark Society, and the City of Rochester. They all expressed support, but none would take it on.[92] It was going to be up to the Susan B. Anthony Memorial and its president to do it.

Howard decided to aim for an endowment of $100,000, an ambitious task that Catt, aware of the difficulty of raising money for women's causes, thought was an overreach.[93] But Howard stood firm. She was reluctant to charge admission to the house, but instead created a "living endowment plan," whereby people from all over the country paid membership fees of up to $5 to the Memorial

The front parlor of the Susan B. Anthony House, where the suffragist was arrested for illegally casting a ballot in the 1872 presidential election. *From the Library of Congress Prints and Photographs Division, Washington, D.C.*

Fund. In pursuit of this goal, she sent out 94 letters in 1945–46 alone.[94] Catt warned her of the poverty of old suffragists: "I think there are at least two [board members] who would find it a very serious matter to even pay a small membership fee."[95] The Foundation received two significant donations. Catt had kept the National American Woman Suffrage Association going because it was to eventually receive a bequest from the Katherine Boyles fund, and when that money became available in 1948, the NAWSA Board voted to contribute $1,000 to the Susan B. Anthony Memorial. In 1950, Susan B. Anthony's birthplace in Adams, Massachusetts, was sold and the house fund received $3,000 from the proceeds.[96] But there were some major disappointments. Two of Howard's strongest supporters, Catt and Mrs. Robert Anderson, led her to believe they would remember the house in their wills, but they both died suddenly in 1947 without doing so.[97]

Raising money for the finite goal of the house purchase proved far easier than collecting a much larger sum for an endowment, and Howard's personal approach for the latter task was less effective. She did not give up hope of large donations; she constantly wrote letters to people she had identified as potential donors, including John D. Rockefeller, Elizabeth Arden, and Bette Davis—none took the bait—and she kept a file of obituaries of wealthy people.[98] The Carnegie and Ford Foundations turned her down.[99] Funding became an ongoing concern. In 1960, there was no money to pay the $25 dues to the National Trust for the Preservation of Historic Places, and in that year the endowment fund stood just over $7,000, far short of the goal she had envisioned.[100] House finances remained a major worry for Howard's successors.

Throughout the campaign, Howard had the support of the Rochester Federation of Women's Clubs and the Anthony Memorial Committee, notably that of Vice President Mrs. W. T. Fulkerson. For the official house opening to the public, the Memorial Committee maintained its annual tradition of honoring Anthony's birthday, planning a "silver" tea on February 14, 1947, with a greatly expanded list of guests, including the mayor and local dignitaries. Everything was in place the night before, except for Catt's portraits, which had not yet arrived. In the afternoon, Howard gave a broadcast about the house on local radio station WHAM and arrived home to find that the pictures would be delivered at 6 p.m. She, her son, and the GI living in the house as a custodian set to work at once and had almost all of them hung by 10:15 that night.

More than 400 visitors arrived on the day of the tea, requiring the hosts to enlist the police to help with traffic. Howard stood in the front parlor wearing a "handsome bombazine of my mother's with a train."[101] Joining her were Mrs. Scott Lyon, President of the Rochester Federation of Women's Clubs; and three members dressed as Susan B. Anthony, Elizabeth Cady Stanton, and Lucretia Mott, with others in the back parlor representing Clara Barton, Frances Willard, and Lucy Stone.[102] The vice-mayor attended (the mayor was out of town), and Governor Thomas E. Dewey sent greetings. Catt, too frail to attend, sent a telegram: "Nothing but good ever came out of the Anthony House. Carry on that tradition."[103] The event raised $300.

Later in the year, Howard took part in a national broadcast over the Columbia network celebrating the anniversary of the Nineteenth Amendment. This was organized by Luella Landin, Howard's personal friend and the radio chairman of the National Council of the General Federation of Women's Clubs.[104] The president of the General Federation spoke first, then Howard, then Georgiana Sibley, a well-respected leader in Rochester society and president of the United Council of Church Women. Sibley spoke on "Challenges of Women Today." Her

Mrs. Florence D. Alexander as Lucy Stone, Mrs. James Bisgrove as Lucretia Mott, and Martha Taylor Howard at dedication of memorial marker on July 22, 1948. *Photograph by Merritt D. Mosher. From the collection of the Local History & Genealogy Division, Rochester Public Library.*

speech was particularly well received, and the program gave the house and Rochester some national recognition.[105]

The following year, as part of the celebrations commemorating the centenary of the July 22, 1848, Seneca Falls Women's Convention, the Susan B. Anthony Memorial Association held a tea and dedication ceremony for a state marker designating the house a historic landmark. The plaque was unveiled by Susan B. Anthony II, herself a well-known women's rights activist.[106] The association also hosted an exhibit for the hundredth anniversary. By this time, the house had become available for events organized by other organizations, such as the Genesee Valley Club's annual tea to raise money for garden upkeep.[107]

Later years

The city and the nation still lacked interest in Susan B. Anthony. Rose Arnold Powell attributed this in part to the fact that Anthony had not attended the convention in Seneca Falls in 1848.[108] Alma Lutz wrote that she was having trouble finding a publisher for her biography: "Publishers have decided that they don't want Susan because they say there is a reaction against women and a book about her won't sell."[109] Howard was not deterred. She was tireless in her promotion of Anthony and the house. She wrote letters to the local newspapers commemorating Anthony's birth and death, reminding readers of important events in the suffrage struggle, celebrating the Nineteenth Amendment and every conceivable occasion that bore relevance to Anthony's life. She also made sure that house events were well-publicized.[110] The local newspapers, the *Democrat and Chronicle* and the *Times-Union*, knew Howard well, appreciated her as a news source, and always published her letters.

In 1946, Howard stepped down as chair of the Rochester Association of Women's Clubs but continued to be president of the Memorial until her death. Her last major campaign was to help get Susan B. Anthony elected to the Hall of Fame for Great Americans, an outdoor sculpture gallery designed by Stanford White and funded in 1900 by Helen Gould, heiress daughter of the robber baron Jay Gould. Candidates for election had to have been native-born, have been deceased for at least twenty-five years, and had to have made a major contribution to the economic, political, or cultural life of the nation. Elections to the Hall of Fame took place every five years; in 1950 there were 118 electors—people "who had achieved a degree of renown," representing every state.[111]

The National Federation of Business and Professional Women's Clubs had been campaigning for Susan B. Anthony's nomination since the 1930s. They came closest in 1945, when, joined by the National Women's Party, the Women's Christian Temperance Union, the DAR, and Rose Arnold Powell, they succeeded in getting Anthony 40 votes, still not enough to qualify.[112]

In 1950, Howard joined the effort. She launched a campaign blitz, getting as many people as possible, many of them men, to write letters to the electors, providing them with a form letter and pointing out that no woman had been elected for thirty years. This time the crusade was successful. Of the six people elected, Susan B. Anthony received 72 votes out of 186, in third place, beating Theodore Roosevelt.[113] With typical modesty, Howard told local journalist Arch Merrill, "Please do not give me any credit about this election and let it all go to the Susan B. Anthony Memorial Inc. I was just the instrument."[114] She was a little chagrined when the National Federation of Business Professionals volunteered to raise $10,000 for the necessary bust and she was not involved.[115] She did not attend the May 1952 ceremony but sent a bouquet of golden gladioli, in honor of the suffrage movement's official color of yellow. The City of Rochester sent lilacs from the Susan B. Anthony bush in Highland Park. Later, on a visit to New York City, Howard went to the Hall of Fame herself with two companions to lay a wreath.[116]

During the 1950s, Howard poured her energy into promoting the interests, visibility, and funding of the house. In 1950, the balance in the house's account was $481, a break-even point but not enough to cover unforeseen expenses. The Rochester Federation of Women's Clubs continued to be a major supporter, with an annual card party raising as much as $200 in 1954, but in the same year coal costs amounted to $300.[117] Howard continued to write letters soliciting memberships; by decade's end there were 500 members.[118]

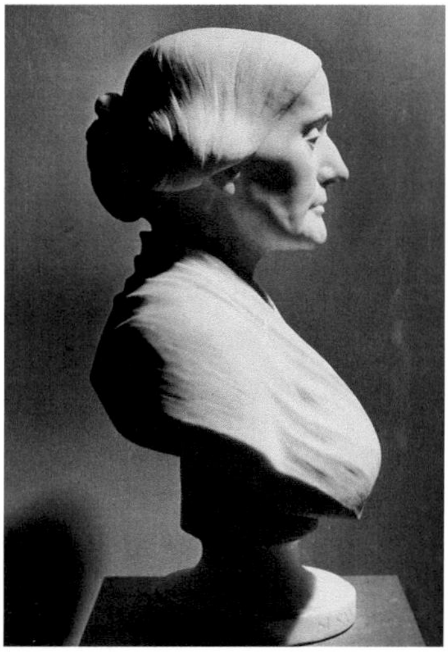

Adelaide Johnson, who sculpted many suffragists, created this portrait bust of Susan B. Anthony. The Hall of Fame bust would be sculpted by Brenda Putnam. *From the collection of the Local History & Genealogy Division, Rochester Public Library.*

Howard received numerous awards for her activism, including Woman of the Year from the Rochester Federation of Women's Clubs, the Good Citizenship Medal from the Rochester Sons of the American Revolution, and the Gold Medal of Honor from the National Society of New England Women. In 1961, she was presented with a medallion at the thirty-eighth Annual Women's International Exposition for "her work in preserving and maintaining the Susan B. Anthony House as a historical place of national importance," and was lauded as "an inspiring example of the true spirit of American patriotism."[119] She also made sure that others received awards. During an interview in 1957, she listed six people she had successfully nominated for awards, including prominent local woman Georgiana Sibley for Mother of the Year.[120]

Howard's domestic life in the 1950s was equally rewarding, especially time spent with her grandchildren. In 1949, her son George Jr. had married Eileen Kern, a World War II veteran and nurse, and they had four children.[121] One of them, Mark, remembers attending Children of the American Revolution meetings and each grandchild getting their own week with Howard. Her granddaughter Christine remembers the occasion when she and older brother Bill dressed in colonial costumes and presented a bouquet to the State Regent at the DAR annual conference at the house. Howard wrote in her Christmas letter for 1961, "Anne [later known as Christine] did the correct curtsy and presented the bouquet and Bill did the correct bow and it gave them experience."[122]

Howard had strong opinions on national and international politics, which were reflected in her membership in the DAR and the local Republican Club. Following the lead of the DAR, she developed a dislike of the United Nations, and, by association, Eleanor Roosevelt, fearing the UN might "be a way of taking us over and having us lose the freedoms we have. I am suspicious of it." Elsewhere she described it as potentially "a gigantic dictatorship."[123] Further influenced by material from the DAR, she also was infected with the Red Scare of the 1950s. She believed that the League of Women Voters had been infiltrated by communists, claiming, "I am a real patriot and I am against all this infiltration. I know all about the subversive work and how people are hoodwinked."[124] When she discovered that Susan B. Anthony II had communist sympathies, she maintained, "If I had known as much about her as I now know, I would not have invited her to unveil the marker here in 1948."[125] She had no high opinion of Susan B. Anthony II even before that. When the great-niece and a companion visited the house in 1947, Howard wrote disparagingly to Alma Lutz: "They were both smoking cigarettes—neither had on stockings—Miss A had toeless shoes—and her nails were stained a deep red—as were her finger nails; high lip coloring." This was uncharacteristically critical. Howard's surviving letters include few personal opinions. She insisted, "I try to think no unkind thoughts of others and I like harmony."[126]

On May 30, 1962, at the age of 86, Howard made remarks and placed a wreath on Susan B. Anthony's grave. In June, she attended her sixty-fifth Mount Holyoke class reunion, and on July 11, she suffered a stroke and was taken to Rochester General Hospital, where she died.[127] Her granddaughter remembered that as a Christian Scientist she was very upset to have been taken to a hospital.[128] Her obituary described her as a "defender of patriotism and people . . . A gentle, soft-spoken little lady, hardly what you'd call an aggressive type . . . but a real tiger when it came to causes to which she was tirelessly dedicated."[129] The Irondequoit chapter of the DAR called her "the Susan B. Anthony of our time."[130] The minutes of the Susan B. Anthony Memorial for September recorded: "Our hearts are filled with sadness and a deep void is evidenced, as our beloved leader is no longer with us. She served us well with loyal devotion and marked energy."[131] Donations to the house in her memory amounted to $276, less than even she might have expected, reflecting the ongoing difficulties in fundraising on women's issues.[132]

Martha Taylor Howard holding a portrait of Susan B. Anthony. She is wearing the ribbons of the Daughters of the American Revolution and the National Society of New England Women. *Photograph: Democrat & Chronicle, June 16, 1957, p. 68. Copyright @Democrat & Chronicle USA TODAY NETWORK*

In her surviving correspondence, Howard did not claim the term feminist, a description that many women avoided in the immediate post-war period.[133] Rose Arnold Powell, another tireless Anthony supporter, *did* embrace the term. Feminism at the time was often linked with leftists and communists, an anathema to middle-class Republican Howard, and she would not have wanted to claim such associations.[134] But Howard epitomized the 1950s' definition of feminism used by Nora Stanton Barney, daughter of Harriot Stanton Blatch, as "one who thinks that women are primarily human beings with the same minds, ambitions, ability and skill, and power for evil and for good as men."[135] Martha Taylor Howard's work was largely local in a conservative middle-class milieu. Yet her achievements were significant. Arriving in Rochester in her sixties as a widow of moderate means, through determination and tact she became a well-recognized and respected figure both in the world of local women's clubs and society at large. A *Democrat & Chronicle* reporter described her in 1962: "Mrs. Howard speaks in cultured New England accents, and you associate her manner with teacups-on-the-knee, crocheted doilies, and antimacassars. But don't let that fool you; the lady is as purposeful as an ICBM missile."[136] Her obituary described the "vast energy and determination" that enabled her to persuade a largely female community to preserve a major landmark in women's history.[137] The Susan B. Anthony House is also a monument to Martha Taylor Howard. ■

1. Martha Taylor Howard (hereafter cited as MTH) to Frederick Hodges, August 23, 1947, Box 245, Folder 8, Susan B. Anthony House Archives (hereafter cited as SBAHA).
2. James Howard, discussion with the author; "She Lives to Serve," Box 246, Folder 42, SBAHA.
3. Rochester *Times-Union,* July 11, 1962, preserved in a scrapbook in Box 57, SBAHA.
4. *Democrat & Chronicle,* June 16, 1957.
5. "Westford Academy," *Wikipedia*, accessed February 8, 2022, https://en.wikipedia.org/wiki/Westford_Academy.
6. Thomas D. Snyder, ed., *120 Years of American Education: A Statistical Portrait* (National Council for Educational Statistics, 1993), 64.
7. Christine Stansell, *The Feminist Promise 1792 to the Present* (New York: The Modern Library, 2011), 108.
8. *Llamarada* (Florence, MA: Bryant Printing Company, 1896, 1897), https://compass.fivecolleges.edu/collections/mount-holyoke-college-collections?islandora_solr_search_navigation=0&f%5B0%5D=catch_all_fields_mt%3A%28Llamarada%29.
9. Ibid.; *Catalogue of Mount Holyoke College, 1899–1900* (Springfield, MA: Springfield Printing and Binding Co., 1899), https://compass.fivecolleges.edu/object/mtholyoke:46327; *Catalogue of Mount Holyoke College, 1902–1903* (Springfield, MA: Springfield Printing and Binding Co., 1902), https://compass.fivecolleges.edu/object/mtholyoke:46330?search=mount%2520holyoke%2520college%2520annual%2520catalog%25201902.
10. Susan Goodier and Karen Pastorello, *Women Will Vote: Winning Suffrage in New York State* (Ithaca, NY: Three Hills, 2017), 116; Jean V. Matthews, *The Rise of the New Woman: The Women's Movement in America, 1875–1930* (Chicago: Ivan R. Dee, 2003), 11, 13.
11. MTH to G. Howard Gould, November 11, 1955, Box 245, Folder 16, SBAHA; Rochester *Times-Union,* July 11, 1962.
12. "The Westford Historical Society and Museum," *Westford Wardsman,* July 2 1917, accessed March 23, 2019, https://museum.westford.org/historic-article/the-westford-wardsman-july-1910/.
13. New England Historic Genealogical Society; Boston, Massachusetts; "Massachusetts Vital Records, 1911–1915," accessed March 23, 2019, https://www.sec.state.ma.us/vitalrecordssearch/vitalrecordssearch.aspx; *Westford Wardsman,* January 6, 1906, October 20, 1906; *Democrat & Chronicle,* January 3, 1962.
14. Minutes of the Executive Committee of the Rochester Federation of Women's Clubs (hereafter cited as RFWC Minutes), October 3, 1944, SBAHA.

15. Christine Bastfield, discussion with the author, May 2, 2019.
16. Christopher Gray, "When Stocks Came in From the Cold," *New York Times*, July 30, 2010.
17. MTH to Mrs. Marjorie Longwell, July 1, 1949, Box 246, Folder 38, SBAHA.
18. U.S. Census Bureau, 1910 US census, population schedule, accessed March 20, 2019, https://www.census.gov.
19. "Wedding,"*Westford Wardsman*, July 2, 1910, August 6, 1910.
20. "New Jersey State Censuses, 1855–1915," The Genealogical Society of New Jersey, accessed February 20, 2022, https://www.gsnj.org/new-jersey-state-censuses/.
21. "Here It Is VTE," *Westford Wardsman*, January 3, 1914; "About Town," *Westford Wardsman*, April 6, 1918; U.S. Census Bureau, [Massachusetts]. [Middlesex].1920 US census, population schedule, accessed March 20, 2019, https://www.census.gov.
22. Mark Howard, discussion with the author.
23. *Democrat & Chronicle*, August 31, 1960.
24. Catherine E. Rymph, *Republican Women: Feminism and Conservatism from Suffrage Through the Rise of the New Right* (Chapel Hill: University of North Carolina Press, 2006), introduction, Kindle.
25. MTH to Mrs. Donaldson, March 1, 1945, Box 246, Folder 43, SBAHA.
26. Mark Howard, discussion.
27. MTH to Alma Lutz, August 26, 1949, Box 246, Folder 38, SBAHA; U.S. Census Bureau, [New York]. [New York].1930 US census, population schedule, accessed March 20, 2019, https://www.census.gov.
28. Winfield Scott Downs, ed., *Encyclopedia of American Biography. New Series: Vol. 3*, s.v. "Howard, George."
29. MTH to Guy Richardson Radley, June 25, 1959, Box 245, Folder 48, SBAHA.
30. MTH to Mrs. Kennt, August 19, 1948, Box 246, Folder 28, SBAHA.
31. MTH to Mrs. Kennt, August 19, 1948, Box 246, Folder 28, SBAHA; MTH to Mrs. Leuscher, October 10, 1957, Box 245, Folder 35, SBAHA.
32. MTH to Guy Richardson Radley, June 25, 1959, Box 245 Folder 48, SBAHA.
33. MTH to Mrs. Arthur Devens Potter, August 12, 1949, Box 246, Folder 38, SBAHA.
34. Manuscript draft, Box 248, Folder 3, SBAHA.
35. Karen J. Blair, *The Clubwoman as Feminist: True Womanhood Redefined, 1869–1914* (New York: Holmes & Meier, 1980), 118; Nancy F. Cott, *The Grounding of Modern Feminism* (New Haven, CT: Yale University Press, 1987), 97; Matthews, *New Woman*, 17.
36. Cott, *Grounding*, 87, 97.
37. Cott, *Grounding*, 94.
38. *Democrat & Chronicle*, June 16, 1957.
39. *Polk's Rochester City Directory, Vol. LXXXX* (Rochester, NY: R. L. Polk & Co., 1940).
40. Christine Bastfield and Mark Howard, discussion.
41. *Democrat & Chronicle*, September 19, 1939; U.S. Census Bureau, [New York]. [Monroe].1940 US census, population schedule, accessed March 20, 2019, https://www.census.gov.
42. *Democrat & Chronicle*, November 19, 1938.
43. Press clipping, Box 246, Folder 42, SBAHA.
44. Newsletter, December 1949, Box 75, Folder 1, SBAHA.
45. *Democrat & Chronicle*, January 22, 1941, April 1, 1941, October 6, 1942, February 11, 1943, July 11,1943; MTH to Rose Arnold Powell, December 2, 1946, Box 246, SBAHA.
46. *Democrat & Chronicle*, July 12, 1962, September 28, 1941, November 20, 1950, June 16, 1957.
47. *Democrat & Chronicle*, July 12, 1962.
48. MTH to the editor, *Christian Science Register*, December 30, 1950, Box 245, Folder 31, SBAHA; MTH to Dr. Lucy Harmon, May 28, 1949, Box 246, Folder 23, SBAHA.
49. *Westford Wardsman*, July 2, 1910.
50. Matthews, *New Woman*, 18.

51. Anna D. Mason to MTH, April 11, 1956, Box 245, Folder 18, SBAHA; MTH to Mrs. Tomlinson, August 1, 1947, Box 246, Folder 3, SBAHA; MTH to Miss Marion May, July 12, 1946, Box 246, Folder 3, SBAHA.
52. Christine Bastfield, discussion.
53. Minutes of the Rochester Federation of Women's Clubs (RFWC), April 1942, July 1942.
54. "Susan B. Anthony, Champion of Women's Rights," Box 244, Folder 1, SBAHA.
55. "Woman of the Week," Box 247, Folder 11, SBAHA; *Democrat & Chronicle*, June 26, 1957.
56. *Democrat & Chronicle*, July 10, 1925; Notes for Arch Merrill, February 26, 1946, Box 246, Folder 26, SBAHA.
57. *Democrat & Chronicle*, February 16, 1929.
58. Susan B. Anthony II, *The Ghost in My Life* (Word Books, 1979), 64.
59. Rose Arnold Powell to MTH, January 2, 1947, Box 247, Folder 27, SBAHA.
60. William Browne to MTH, Box 246, Folder 11, SBAHA.
61. RFWC Minutes, May 12, 1944, SBAHA.
62. "Story of the Susan B. Anthony House," (hereafter cited as "House Story"), 1, Box 247, Folder 14, SBAHA.
63. "House Story," 1–2.
64. RFWC Minutes, November 10, 1944, April 13, 1945, SBAHA; "House Story," 2–3, SBAHA.
65. Mary Anthony information for Albany memorial, Box 254, Folder "Katherine Thompson," SBAHA.
66. MTH to Carrie Chapman Catt, November 1, 1946, Box 246, Folder 23, SBAHA.
67. MTH to Alma Lutz, undated, Box 246, Folder 7, SBAHA.
68. "Mrs. Danforth passes at 97," *Democrat & Chronicle*, May 21, 1961.
69. Elswyth Thane, *Mount Vernon Is Ours* (New York: Duell, Sloan and Pearce, 1966), 448.
70. MTH to Miss Smith, July 5, 1947, Box 246, Folder 20, SBAHA.
71. "House Story," 3, Box 247, Folder 14, SBAHA.
72. MTH to Rose Arnold Powell, December 26, 1946, Box 246, Folder 2, SBAHA; MTH to Mr. Riges, December 6, 1955, Box 245, Folder 13, SBAHA.
73. MTH to Miss Smith, July 5, 1947, Box 246, Folder 20, SBAHA; "House Story," 2, SBAHA.
74. MTH to Carrie Chapman Catt, August 2, 1946, Box 26, Folder 20, SBAHA.
75. RFWC Minutes, April 13, 1945, SBAHA.
76. Box 246, Folder 8, SBAHA.
77. Willard Leuscher Papers, Box 253, Folder 4, SBAHA.
78. Ibid.
79. MTH to Mrs. Howe, November 19, 1945, Box 246, Folder 9, SBAHA; "House Story," 3.
80. Eleanor Gleason to MTH, August 3, 1945; Kodak to MTH, May 10, 1945, Box 246, Folder 15, SBAHA.
81. MTH to Mrs. Kitchelt, January 19, 1946, Box 246, Folder 20, SBAHA.
82. Willard Leuscher papers, Box 253, Folder 4, SBAHA.
83. MTH to Rose Arnold Powell, December 2, 1946, Box 246, Folder 2, SBAHA.
84. MTH to Carrie Chapman Catt, August 23, 1945, Box 246, Folder 17, SBAHA.
85. "House Story," 6–7.
86. MTH to the Trustees of the Susan B. Anthony Memorial, n.d., Box 246, Folder 3, SBAHA; "Items About the Anthony House," Box 245, Folder 20, SBAHA.
87. Leila J. Rupp & Verta Taylor, *Survival in the Doldrums: The American Women's Rights Movement 1945 to the 1960s* (Columbus, OH: Ohio State University Press, 1990), 47.
88. Rupp & Taylor, *Survival*, 115; MTH to Florence Kitchelt, January 15, 1946, Box 246, Folder 20, SBAHA.
89. "House Story," 6.
90. "House Story," 7–8; MTH to Rose Arnold Powell, December 2, 1946, Box 246, Folder 2, SBAHA.
91. RFWC Minutes, March 9, 1945, SBAHA.

92. "Who'll Take Lead to Preserve Anthony Home?" *Democrat & Chronicle*, February 15, 1945.
93. Carrie Chapman Catt to MTH, May 23, 1945, Box 246, Folder 25, SBAHA.
94. Box 246, Folder 26, SBAHA.
95. "House Story," 10; Minutes of the Susan B. Anthony Memorial Inc., June 6, 1945, Box 256, Folder 1, SBAHA; Carrie Chapman Catt to MTH, October 22, 1946, October 1, 1946, Box 246, Folders 25, 43, SBAHA.
96. Box 246, Folder 23, SBAHA.
97. MTH to Alma Lutz, July 22, 1948, Box 246, Folder 38, SBAHA.
98. MTH to Carrie Chapman Catt, August 26, 1946; MTH to Alice Paul, January 19, 1946, Box 246, Folder 20, SBAHA.
99. MTH's notes on back of UN News for Women Broadcasters, Box 246, Folder 3, SBAHA.
100. Yearly report, 1959–60, Box 245, Folder 35, SBAHA.
101. MTH to Rose Arnold Powell, March 3,1947, Box 245, Folder 27, SBAHA.
102. Press release for Women's Press Club, February 14, 1947, Box 245, Folder 4, SBAHA.
103. MTH to Carrie Chapman Catt, February 21, 1947, Box 246, Folder 3, SBAHA; Press release for the Women's Press Club, Box 245, Folder 4, SBAHA.
104. MTH to Carrie Chapman Catt, August 23, 1945, Box 246, Folder 17, SBAHA.
105. MTH to Carrie Chapman Catt, August 23, 1945; MTH to Mrs. Sibley, August 26, 1945, Box 246, Folder 17, SBAHA.
106. Albert B. Corey to MTH, June 28, 1948, Box 246, Folder 4, SBAHA.
107. Visit by Marjorie Taylor Longwell, Box 246, Folder 8, SBAHA.
108. Rose Arnold Powell to MTH, November 12, 1948, Box 246, Folder 10, SBAHA.
109. Alma Lutz to MTH, March 23, 1948, August 9, 1948, Box 246, Folder 7, SBAHA.
110. Draft of letter to the editor of the *Democrat & Chronicle*, November 1945, Box 246, Folder 26, SBAHA.
111. Records of the Hall of Fame of Great Americans, "Historical Note," New York University Archives, accessed February 20, 2022, http://dlib.nyu.edu/findingaids/html/archives/halloffame/bioghist.html
112. Kate Culkin, "Aunt Susan's Place," *New York Archives*, accessed February 20, 2022, Aunt Susan's Place (nysarchivestrust.org); MTH to Mrs. Robert Anderson, May 4, 1945, Box 246, Folder 30, SBAHA.
113. MTH to Gertrude Conway (Editor of DAR Magazine), November 15, 1950, Box 245, Folder 31, SBAHA; Minutes of Susan B. Anthony Memorial, November 2, 1950, Box 256, Folder 2, SBAHA; *Democrat & Chronicle*, November 2, 1950.
114. MTH to Arch Merrill, n.d., Box 245, Folder 33, SBAHA.
115. Alma Lutz to MTH, February 28, 1951, Box 248, Folder 3, SBAHA; MTH to Arch Merrill, February 28, 1951, Box 248, Folder 3, SBAHA.
116. Christmas letter, Box 254, Folder 2, SBAHA; *Democrat & Chronicle*, November 2, 1961.
117. Susan B. Anthony Memorial Association account books, 1954–55, Box 62, SBAHA.
118. Form letter to prospective donors, Box 246, Folder 33, SBAHA.
119. Program, 38th Annual Women's International Exposition, November 1961, Box 246, Folder 31, SBAHA.
120. *Democrat & Chronicle*, June 16, 1957.
121. *Democrat & Chronicle*, February 13, 1949; December 4, 1985.
122. Christine Bastfield and Mark Howard, discussion; Christmas letter, Box 254, Folder 2, SBAHA.
123. MTH to Mrs. McCann, December 4, 1955, Box 245, Folder 13, SBAHA; Press clipping, August 21, 1945, Box 527, Folder 14, SBAHA.
124. MTH to Mrs. Waite, September 25, 1955, Box 245, Folder 16, SBAHA.
125. MTH to Daniel Anthony, n.d., Box 245, Folder 28, SBAHA; MTH to Alma Lutz, Box 245, Folder 12, SBAHA; Susan B. Anthony II, *Ghost*, 171.

126. MTH to Alma Lutz, August 22, 1947, Box 245, Folder 12, SBAHA; MTH to Mrs. Waite, September 24, 1955, Box 245, Folder 16, SBAHA.
127. Memorial Day program in private collection of Mark Howard; *Democrat & Chronicle*, July 12, 1962.
128. Christine Bastfield, discussion.
129. *Democrat & Chronicle*, July 12, 1962.
130. *Democrat & Chronicle*, August 4, 1962.
131. Minutes of Susan B. Anthony Memorial, September 6, 1962, Box 256, Folder 3, SBAHA.
132. [130] Box 259, Folder 3, SBAHA.
133. Rupp & Taylor, *Survival*, 52.
134. Ellen Schrecker, *Many Are the Crimes: McCarthyism in America* (Boston: Little, Brown and Company, 1999), 386–87.
135. Rupp & Taylor, *Survival*, 52, 54.
136. *Democrat & Chronicle*, April 22, 1960.
137. *Democrat & Chronicle*, July 11, 1962, Box 57, Folder 94.1.630, SBAHA.

Laura Warren Hill Discusses 'Strike the Hammer'

In these edited excerpts from an interview by RIT history professor Tamar Carroll and history major Caitlin McCabe, Laura Warren Hill discusses the sources she used to write Strike the Hammer: The Black Freedom Struggle in Rochester, New York, 1940–1970 *(Cornell University Press, 2021), including more than forty original oral history interviews. She also talks about what was distinctive about Black migration to Rochester, the significance of Black capitalism, and how studying Rochester can change broader understandings of the civil rights movement and the African American experience in the mid-twentieth century.*

Carroll: *What was the origin of this book?*
Hill: I started off thinking that I was just going to be writing about the uprising of July 1964. As it turned out, when I started to interview folks from the city, when I started to really get into the archives, I learned that the history that came before [the uprising] was, in some cases, far more interesting that the history of that event itself. And that the organizing tradition that grew out of the uprising had some really important national implications.

Carroll: *Can you tell us a little bit about the sources that you used to get at that story?*
Hill: The University of Rochester has an incredible archive, starting with Minister Franklin Florence's papers. Minister Florence was the president of the FIGHT [Freedom, Independence, God, Honor, Today] organization essentially from its inception. The University of Rochester also has a collection on what they titled the "1964 Race Riot." I wouldn't use the language "riot," but in the kind of historical parlance, that is the term that gets used.

I also used a number of clipping files from the [Rochester] Public Library's Local History Division. They had a really incredible set of materials on Malcolm X and the time he spent in the city and some of the organizing work that he helped to do. Really, it's less that he helped organize and more that he brought national attention to the organizing that was happening in Rochester around some police brutality cases that took place in advance of the uprising. . . . The files of Mayor [Frank] Lamb and City Manager Porter Homer were both available in the City archives, and so I used a good deal of that work as well.

I did an oral history interview project where we interviewed somewhere between 40 and 50 people who were in and around Rochester and either working as activists or [were] people who were able to testify to the conditions in the city during the time of the uprising and throughout the organizing that took place afterwards.

I also took advantage of a number of local publications. The city historian, Blake McKelvey, wrote for years about Rochester's past. While I didn't always see eye to eye with some of his interpretations, I did draw heavily on his research and some of the work that he had done. Finally, a couple of local historians wrote really incredible pieces on the southern migrants who came up to Rochester every year to work in the orchards and the fields surrounding the city of Rochester, and they documented what that process was like. To get a feel for who was migrating to Rochester in the years leading up to the uprising, I really relied on other historians.

Carroll: *Can you tell us about what you learned from the oral histories that you did?*

Hill: In terms of the research and Rochester, I think one of the things I took away was how, despite the differences that existed among the various people that make up Black Rochester, there was an incredible sense of unity at particular moments in the city's history, and that's what allowed a kind of organizing tradition to take root at this particular moment and to really explode.

I learned a great deal about the inner workings of social movements. Often when we think of social movements, we think about protest. Maybe if we're a little more open minded, [we] think about uprisings or rebellions as a form of social movement. But, in truth, those are just moments. They cannot sustain a movement. We frequently see on TV and other places . . . those moments, but what we don't see is the day-to-day work, that in and out, planning and organizing people, and, in most cases, the work that women do behind the scenes that never makes it into the newspapers or onto the nightly news, and that is the kind of organizing work of bringing people together.

The FIGHT organization was an umbrella organization that was made up of many other organizations. Some of those other organizations existed at the time of the uprising; many of them did not. In large part, it was women getting out into the streets, going back to their communities, going to their neighborhoods, and organizing the people that they knew, to get them to have a voice and an active role in this larger social movement, in this larger FIGHT organization.

Carroll: *When you said that there was incredible unity in the Black community in Rochester, would you say that unity was based around a sense of a need for change in terms of economic inequality, housing discrimination, and police brutality?*

Hill: Where I saw the most unity was around the issue of police brutality. And this is in large part because the differences that might have worked to separate members of the Black community were irrelevant when it came to dealing with the police. . . . If you were Black in Rochester, you were under suspicion.

There were also issues with housing. For everybody who lived in the spaces that made up Black Rochester at the time, they faced a consistent housing crisis. They paid more for their rent than most other people in the city did, and they often got less for it. And when you're talking about housing restrictions, you're also talking about access to schools, to playgrounds, to grocery stores, to shopping centers, to public transportation. And so it goes much beyond housing into the kind of community access that is available to you, and so that was absolutely another condition that created considerable unity.

Carroll: *In some ways, what you just described sounds similar to Harlem or Detroit in terms of the Great Migration and the social and economic conditions that Black migrants to northern cities faced. But you also write about ways in which Rochester was distinctive.*

Hill: One of the things that we know about the Great Migration is that it occurred in two main waves, concurrent with the World Wars. The migration that really had an impact on Rochester was in that second wave between 1940 and 1970. Unlike the migrants that were going to New York City or to Los Angeles or Detroit, where there were manufacturing industries that were in desperate need of their labor, Rochester was not in desperate need of their labor in manufacturing. Not only were they not in need of it, they didn't want it. [But there was] a labor shortage in the fields, and so agricultural workers from the South—from places like Sanford, Florida, were recruited to come up and work in the agricultural industry in Rochester, as opposed to manufacturing or wartime defense industry positions.

This had a real impact on how those migrants experienced Rochester and how Rochester chose to experience those migrants. Importantly, there was an educational difference. Many of the migrants that were coming to work in the fields didn't have a high school education because they were constantly working in the agricultural industry. In places like Rochester, Kodak and Xerox both had a requirement that all employees have a high school diploma. So if you did not have that high school diploma, it didn't matter what the job was—how simple or easy or repetitive—it meant you simply couldn't get hired into those places.

So when the agricultural migrants decided that they wanted to stay in Rochester, they didn't want to continue working in agriculture, [but] there weren't necessarily other fields for them to move into. This created a large number of unemployed Black folks in the City of Rochester. . . . The other thing was the migrant nature, the agricultural work, allowed white Rochester to stigmatize them as uneducated and disorganized.

Carroll: *How did this research change what you thought you knew about the uprising?*

Hill: When we study local movements, what we learn is not just important in those local communities, but it can tell us a whole lot about what was happening nationally as well. It was really important in Rochester that the Nation of Islam, popularly called the Black Muslims, worked closely with the NAACP to fight police brutality. In doing the archival work, I found that the NAACP national branch was really, really angry at the Rochester branch for working with the Nation of Islam. They saw this kind of local collaboration as potentially dangerous for their national fundraising.

There is some really interesting conflict between local branches and the national organizations of social movements. A lot of times we hear about what the national organization did and that becomes the write-in for the organization as a whole, when really there was so much happening in these local areas that is worth our study as well.

On the national stage, we hear a tremendous amount about ministers in the civil rights movement. There's this kind of sense that Christians were behind the civil rights movement. Nobody is talking about that in the Black Power movement. Except in Rochester what emerges as Black Power was led by Black ministers. . . . This idea that there was a transition from civil rights, which was nonviolent, to Black Power, which was militant and aggressive, just isn't really the story that happened in places like Rochester. It's not that neat or that clean.

Another important thing that came out of my research is the way the Black community in Rochester worked with Saul Alinsky and E.D. Chambers and the Industrial Areas Foundation to really leverage the financial well-being that the national churches had and to leverage the national media spotlight to bring attention to what happened in Rochester to really move Eastman Kodak. And here, I'm referring to the shareholder proxy strategy that the FIGHT organization pulled off. And that shareholder strategy, although not original to the FIGHT organization, was really the first successful public example of how that could be used against a Fortune 500 company like Eastman Kodak. It would later go on to be used in the anti-apartheid movement in South Africa and others like it. So Rochester had such an outsized impact on that period in history and certainly on how social movements were operating in what we call the long 1960s.

Carroll: *There are many things that are important about your book, but if you had to pinpoint, what would you say your central argument is?*

Hill: I was really trying to show how an outnumbered, relatively powerless group of people navigated conflict with those in power in ways that were successful. . . . It's really in those kinds of examples that we have to look for [ways] to challenge power, how to challenge systemic and institutional injustice. What folks in Rochester were really trying to do was operate at a systemic and institutional level. They were not content to challenge individual acts of racism.

They did that, too, but that could not be the end of what they did. They really saw in the Black Power movement an opportunity to create structures, to create institutions, that would not replicate or repeat what happened in white America but that could function alongside white America and really serve the Black community. An example of this is the partnership between the FIGHT organization and Xerox that led to the creation of one of the nation's first community development corporations, whereby the Black community would own and operate a business, an industry, really, and they would partner with local industries to serve the needs of the Black community.

McCabe: *You write about Black capitalism, and I think it's a really unique aspect of Rochester at this time. Where do you think that comes out of? And where do you think Black capitalism fits into our modern conception of the civil rights movement?*

Hill: I wouldn't say it's actually even

unique in [that] moment. I'm just one of the first people to kind of focus on it. But the Nation of Islam was absolutely into Black capitalism. They were absolutely into using forms of Black capitalism to promote and preserve their way of life, this kind of notion of doing for self. But that's not new, either. It wasn't original to the Nation of Islam; they were just kind of the mid-century repository for that kind of mode of thinking.

One of the things that we see in Rochester is that communal entrepreneurial economic spirit, and you can go back through and look at the post-Civil War period in the US. Black folks were excluded from insurance agencies, and so they formed their own communal societies where folks put in five cents a month, or whatever they could put in, and then, when somebody in their family died, the widow was taken care of, the people were buried.

That tradition of communal support is really deep in the Black tradition, and so what happens in Rochester in the long 1960s is that there's an effort for Black folks to become industrial producers. To not just have mom-and-pop stores, to not just engage in small business, but to try to transcend to that larger scale [of] operating that companies like Kodak are doing, because they recognize that a mom-and-pop shop supports a family. What they wanted was some kind of Black company that could support a community, and so that's where we see a kind of development in this era.

Folks in Cleveland were trying to do this a different way; they were trying to franchise McDonald's to provide an income and jobs and security to the Black community.[1] Again, it's not necessarily unique to Rochester; it's just that this is one of the first books that really kind of tackles that very self-consciously. It's also important to keep in mind that Black Power organizations at this time were really more invested in a socialist way of thriving economically than a capitalist way, and so Black capitalism became kind of like a dirty word in the Black Power movement, but that's another narrative that is changing with the newer generation of scholarship.

Carroll: *It's interesting, because when we think about the Southern civil rights movement, those are more consumer-based. And so, to think about Rochester really targeting the corporations and the means of production . . .*
Hill: Absolutely, and I think that's really a perfect kind of distinction that I'm trying to make is that, in the civil rights movement, you really do see Black folks using consumption protest. They're using their power, as consumers, to try to force a change. What happens in this moment is that Black folks are saying, "Being a consumer is to constantly be on the defensive end, but if we can become producers, if we can control the means of production, then we're in the driver's seat. We're not subject to what white capital does or tells us or allows us; we get to be in charge of this."

Carroll: *I am excited to see what kind of new directions this is going to lead historians across the US in.*
Hill: One thought that I would like to leave you and your readers with is that this type of work, and by work I mean my own work, the kind of labor that I did to bring this story to print, is not something that can be done by an individual or in isolation. All of the ideas that come to the fore in this book were discussed and debated and negotiated with other historians, with my interview subjects, with multiple

communities. Too often we think about the writing of history as an isolated or solitary act.

I'm frequently uncomfortable by the kind of attribution I get for this story. It is not my story. I could never have written this book without the assistance of the people who did the work that I'm writing about or my fellow scholars and community members and activists who really worked through ideas with me. So, I just want to say that history can't happen in a vacuum. It has got to happen in dialogue and conversation. ■

1.Marcia Chatelain, *Franchise: The Golden Arches in Black America* (New York: Norton, 2020).

BOOK REVIEW

Strike the Hammer: The Black Freedom Struggle in Rochester, New York, 1940–1970

by Laura Warren Hill. Ithaca, NY: Cornell University Press, 2021.

Michael Brown, Rochester Institute of Technology

In February 1963, Baden Street Settlement in northeast Rochester was the site of a mass meeting to protest discriminatory, brutal policing in Rochester. Among recent outrages was the beating of Rufus Fairwell, a Black service-station worker who was confronted by two white police officers as he closed up shop. Though wearing his work uniform and producing keys to the business, Fairwell was arrested with such violence that two of his vertebrae were broken.[1]

The six-hundred-plus people gathered at Baden heard powerful messages from leaders local and national. "My people have caught hell long enough," Malcolm X declared. In order to make change, it was time to "let the man know that you are fed up." Mildred Johnson, a Baden Street neighborhood leader and vice president of the Negro Business and Professional Women's Organization, called Rochester "the Mississippi of New York State." Dr. Walter Cooper, chairing the meeting on behalf of the local NAACP, observed that Rochester "may well be at the crossroads in race relations."[2]

Cooper was right. Seventeen months later, the compounding moral and material injuries of racially discriminatory housing, schooling, employment, and policing resulted in an uprising of Black residents that shook Rochester. It began not far from Baden Street.

The uprising of July 24–26, 1964, has loomed large for Rochesterians. It was the subject of an excellent 2006 documentary by local filmmakers Carvin Eison and Chris Christopher. It was marked by extensive reporting in the Rochester *CITY* and *Democrat & Chronicle* newspapers on its fortieth anniversary in 2004 and again on its fiftieth in 2014. Photographs from those three days are many and vivid. They show columns of helmeted police and, ultimately, the National Guard patrolling the city's streets. Martin Luther King Jr.

told the press that "If law and order are to be maintained in New York City, Rochester, or Mississippi, it can be done when there is an ever-increasing measure of justice and dignity accorded all persons."[3] It is no wonder that the uprising continues to command attention.

In *Strike the Hammer*, however, Laura Warren Hill demonstrates the need to look not only at but also beyond those July days, training our vision on the organizing, activism, and struggles that both preceded and followed 1964. The 1960s are a middle decade in her examination of a long "Black freedom struggle" in Rochester, which she traces from 1940 to 1970.

Hill's wider focus serves to reposition the 1964 uprising. It came after a host of organized reform efforts, of which the 1963 mass meeting at Baden Street is but one example. One month after that meeting, the Democratic majority on Rochester City Council voted to establish a civilian Police Advisory Board (PAB) to hear and investigate claims of "excessive or unnecessary force." That PAB, whose acronym was revived in 2019 with the latest iteration of Rochester's Police Accountability Board, was the result of considerable organizing on its behalf. Five hundred people had attended a hearing on the proposed board, with sixty-seven of them speaking. The *Democrat & Chronicle* reported that those in favor included "minority groups," clergy from "all three faiths," and "labor leaders." In its first year, the PAB received twenty complaints but dismissed eighteen of them as beyond its purview. Though seven of these complaints fell precisely within the jurisdiction of the board—allegations of "unnecessary use of force"—they were rejected on such grounds as occurring before the ordinance establishing the PAB was passed or, in four cases, failure to properly authorize paperwork.[4]

In short, Black Rochesterians in the years before 1964 had effectively assembled a broad reform coalition to confront institutional racism in the city. They worked through the regular channels of city government, settlement houses, and faith groups. These herculean labors generated results, such as the PAB, which were—in the face of withering obstruction and opposition—modest at best. The 1964 uprising occurred only after such efforts had proven unable to substantially alter conditions in Rochester.

By providing an account of the Rochester Black freedom struggle that highlights generations of leaders, tactical shifts, and strategic coalitions from 1940 on, Hill successfully challenges a view of 1964 that arose in its immediate aftermath and has endured. As she puts it: "When accounts of the Rochester uprising circulated nationally in 1964, any mention of Black agency, community formation, organization, or leadership were truncated or omitted in favor of narratives about Black disorder and pathology. Told that way, Black Rochester appeared disorganized, chaotic, lacking in leadership, and unable to identify and name its oppression. Nothing was further from the truth."[5]

In the context of Hill's research, what happened in Rochester in 1964 was not simply a riot that broke out on a hot summer night; it was a rebellion years in the making.

Hill's work on Rochester fits into a wider historiographical reevaluation of urban unrest in the 1960s. Historian Heather Ann Thompson may be known to readers for her 2016 Pulitzer Prize-winning book, *Blood in the Water: The Attica Prison Uprising of 1971 and Its Legacy*. Earlier in her career, she identified two competing views of the 1960s in historical writing. These views, she observed, began from fundamentally different questions: "Did the urban violence of the 1960s stem merely from reckless "riots," which served primarily to undermine postwar political stability and erode the existing possibilities for inner-city vitality? Or were they reasonable "rebellions" intended to call attention to the continuing inequality in these same urban centers?"[6]

Assessing the work of historians Arnold Hirsch, James Ralph, and Thomas Sugrue on the decade's uprisings, Thompson concluded that "the preponderant evidence in their works suggests that rebellion is exactly what they were."[7] Since Thompson wrote, that body of historical scholarship has only grown.

The sheer scale and widespread geographic distribution of urban unrest is a crucial part of the picture historians have drawn. Historian Elizabeth Hinton has recently pointed out that in the period 1964–72 there was violence "not only in archetypal ghettoes including Harlem and Watts, in majority-Black cities such as Detroit and Washington, DC," but also "in Greensboro, North Carolina, in Gary, Indiana, in Seattle, Washington, and countless places in between—every city, small or large, where Black residents lived in segregated, unequal conditions."[8]

In addition to positioning Rochester within this broader national story, *Strike the Hammer* plays an important part in ongoing, multifaceted efforts to change local understandings of the city's history. In 2020, for example, the City Roots Community Land Trust and the Yale Environmental Protection Clinic issued *Confronting Racial Covenants: How They Segregated Monroe County and What To Do About Them.*[9] This report details how deed restrictions were one of several tactics used to prevent the sale of properties to Black buyers in metropolitan Rochester. Though the Supreme Court blocked the enforcement of such covenants in 1948, they remained literally on the books. In December 2020, neighbors in the Meadowbrook tract of the Rochester suburb Brighton took action to remove racial covenants from the deeds of 288 homes.[10]

A second new book on Rochester history complements *Strike the Hammer* and could be read in tandem with it. *Your Children Are Very Greatly in Danger: School Segregation in Rochester* by *Democrat & Chronicle* education reporter Justin Murphy details the struggle for and entrenched opposition to racially integrated schools from the time of Frederick Douglass to the present.[11]

A further effort is taking shape at Baden Park, a few yards from Baden Street Settlement, where the 1963 mass meeting took place. There, the Spiritus Anti-Racism Coalition (SPARC) has taken the lead in planning the future Minister Franklin Florence Civil Rights Heritage Site. SPARC, with leadership from the Reverend Myra Brown of Spiritus Christi Church, envisions the site as "an outdoor civil rights heritage classroom."[12]

Franklin Florence appears on *Strike The Hammer*'s cover. He was the first chairperson of FIGHT (Freedom, Independence, God, Honor, Today), the most ambitious community organization forged by Black Rochesterians after the 1964 uprising. He stands among protestors at Kodak's 1967 shareholder meeting in Flemington, New Jersey, where he and FIGHT pressed the company to open its notoriously closed doors to Black job seekers.[13] Clad in tan raincoat, black sunglasses, white shirt, and black tie, Florence is flanked by a sign that reads: "Broken Promises Hot Summer."

The heightened degree of organization and confrontation on display in Flemington were, Hill argues, a result of new avenues for action that followed 1964. That year's "rising," she writes, "served as a fundamental precondition for the transformation of the [city's] Black freedom movement." In Rochester, "the Black community quite literally struck for equality, self-determination, and economic advancement while the iron was still hot from the 1964 rebellion."[14]

Amid an ongoing pandemic in which the burden of death has fallen most heavily on people of color and working-class Americans, and following mass protests as well as considerable political mobilization in the names of Daniel Prude and others, the iron is hot again. Hill's book and the many complementary efforts to raise consciousness of Rochester's history are vital resources for a community asking, "Where do we go from here?" ■

1. Justin Murphy, "Attempts at Reforming Rochester Police Have a 50-year History. All Have Fallen Short," Rochester *Democrat & Chronicle* online, April 7, 2021, https://www.democratandchronicle.com/story/news/2021/04/07/rochester-ny-police-reform-history-half-century-attempts-civil-lawsuit-daniel-prude/7063360002/.
2. Walter Cooper, "7.24.64, Reflections on the Rochester Riots," Rochester *City Newspaper*, July 21, 2004, https://www.rochestercitynewspaper.com/rochester/72464/Content?oid=2129083; Bill Vogler, "Negroes Call for Unity to Protest 'Abuses,'" *Democrat & Chronicle*, February 18, 1963, 15.
3. Clip number wsbn46951, WSB-TV news film clip of Dr. Martin Luther King Jr. speaking about race riots in Rochester and New York City, New York, 1964, July 27, WSB-TV news film collection, reel 1187, 51:25/57:31, Walter J. Brown Media Archives and Peabody Awards Collection, The University of Georgia Libraries, Athens, Georgia, http://crdl.usg.edu/id:ugabma_wsbn_wsbn46951.
4. Pat Brasley, "Democrats Agree to Form City Policy Advisory Board," *Democrat & Chronicle*, March 16, 1963, 1, 5; Brasley, "Council Okays Advisory Board On Party Vote," *Democrat & Chronicle*, March 27, 1963, 1, 5; "Business' Slow for Police Board," *Democrat & Chronicle*, August 8, 1964, 6A; "Year's Score: 2 Cases for Police Board," Rochester *Times-Union*, August 7, 1964, scan posted by "R-IMC" on April 21, 2015 to http://rochester.indymedia.org/node/146865.
5. Laura Warren Hill, *Strike the Hammer: The Black Freedom Struggle in Rochester, New York, 1940–1970* (Ithaca, NY: Cornell University Press, 2021), 11.
6. Heather Ann Thompson, "Urban Uprisings: Riots or Rebellions?" in David Farber and Beth Bailey, eds., *The Columbia Guide to America in the 1960s* (New York: Columbia University Press, 2003), 110.
7. Thompson, 115.
8. Elizabeth Hinton, *America on Fire: The Untold History of Police Violence and Black Rebellion Since the 1960s* (New York: W. W. Norton and Company, 2021), 2–3.
9. City Roots Community Land Trust and the Yale Environmental Protection Clinic, *Confronting Racial Covenants: How They Segregated Monroe County and What to Do About Them* (City Roots Community Land Trust, 2020), https://law.yale.edu/sites/default/files/area/clinic/document/2020.7.31_-_confronting_racial_covenants_-_yale.city_roots_guide.pdf.
10. Sean Lahman, "Racial Covenants Removed from Deeds in Brighton Neighborhood after 90 Years," *Democrat & Chronicle* online, December 18, 2020, https://www.democratandchronicle.com/story/news/2020/12/18/racial-convenants-removed-300-deeds-brighton-neighborhood/3944085001/.

11. Justin Murphy, *Your Children Are Very Greatly in Danger: School Segregation in Rochester, New York* (Ithaca, NY: Cornell University Press, 2022).
12. Natalia Rodriguez Medina, "How You Can Participate in Black History Month Events in Rochester," *Democrat & Chronicle* online, February 10, 2022, https://www.democratandchronicle.com/story/news/2022/02/07/black-history-month-events-rochester-ny-2022/6654309001/; Spiritus Christi Church, "SPARC: Spiritus Anti-Racism Coalition," https://spirituschristi.org/spiritusministries/sparc/, accessed March 8, 2022.
13. Justin Murphy, "George Eastman Created Rochester's Middle Class. Why Was the Black Community Left Behind?" *Democrat and Chronicle* online, June 10, 2021, https://www.democratandchronicle.com/in-depth/news/2021/06/07/george-eastman-kodak-rochester-ny-legacy-black-race-relations-philanthropy/4755198001/.
14. Hill, 5, 4.

REVIEW ESSAY

Attica Revisited

Shanleigh Corrallo, University at Buffalo

The fiftieth anniversary of the 1971 Attica Prison Rebellion arrived during a time pregnant with tense conversations on mass incarceration, criminal justice reform, racial (in)justice, and police brutality. The George Floyd protests of 2020 ushered in urgent conversations on the inequities wrought within our nation's policing structure and, at the most fundamental level, highlighted the racial tensions that continue to divide our country. Most poignantly, the remembrance of the Attica Prison Rebellion occurred during a crossroads of policing. Building from historical precedent of Black community resistance against police brutality, activists have called for an overhaul of the police structure through renewed citizen oversight committees (with vested disciplinary power), divestment from police budgets to reinvest in social, behavioral, and mental health services; police accountability for use-of-force incidents; and data transparency, among other platforms. Governments have responded mostly with piecemeal legislation and programmatic adjustments that keep systems status quo, although some notable changes have been made.[1]

Open Wounds: The 50-Year Legacy of the Attica Prison Uprising and Local Connections, Central Library of Rochester & Monroe County. Traveling exhibit curated by staff at the New York State Museum, with local content by Chris Christopher, Gary Craig, and Christine L. Ridarsky. September 1, 2021–January 28, 2022.

Attica. Stanley Nelson and Traci A. Curry, directors and producers; Vinnie Malhotra, Marcia Smith, and Jihan Robinson, executive producers. Firelight Films, 2021. Premiered on Showtime, November 6, 2021. 116 Minutes.

For New Yorkers, and especially Western New Yorkers, Attica is an omnipresent trauma. Generations have yet to heal because the very forces that enabled the slaughter of thirty-nine prisoners and four correctional officers on September 13, 1971, still exist today. This was vividly exposed in 2020 with the murder of Daniel Prude, a forty-one-year-old Black male who was experiencing a mental health episode and died while being constrained by Rochester police officers. The tragic police killings of George Floyd, Breonna Taylor, Rayshard Brooks, and Daniel Prude ripped open the wound of Attica because they evidenced issues identical to those protested across the country in the 1960s. Massive community uprisings against police brutality in Rochester (1964) and Buffalo (1967) were ignited by police brutality incidents. Grassroots organizations like FIGHT

(Freedom, Integrity, God, Honor, Today) in Rochester and BUILD (Build Unity, Independence, Leadership and Dignity) in Buffalo organized residents to demand police accountability. FIGHT and BUILD both eventually played a part in the Attica Rebellion, bringing their local expertise to the internationally publicized drama.

Simultaneously, prisoners inside New York State's "correctional" institutions implemented Black Power ideologies and philosophies to resist abuse and demand humane treatment. Less than a year before Attica, prisoners at Auburn Correctional Facility—just outside of Syracuse—took control over the prison and held more than fifty hostages.[2] The impetus behind prisoners' Rebellions at Auburn and Attica were identical: Treat us like human beings. In both Auburn and Attica, prisoners were inspired by the Civil Rights and Black Power movements nationally and locally; they used this as momentum to refuse continued brutalization and to reject "the unmitigated oppression wrought by the racist administrative network of this prison throughout the year."[3]

The profundity of Attica as a resilient historical moment with undeniable modern connections has led to a flurry of commemorative events, media, talks, and even technology. The reshuffling of historical actors—highlighting the local, while remembering the state and national—when revisiting Attica, is an overarching theme in several key commemorations of Attica, including the Showtime documentary *Attica* and "Open Wounds: The 50-Year Legacy of the Attica Prison Uprising," the New York State Museum's traveling poster exhibit, with local content developed to complement its installation in Rochester Although each project is distinct in format and facilitation, they all contribute new perspectives on the Attica Rebellion.

Several common themes between *Attica*, directed by Stanley Nelson and Traci A. Curry, and "Open Wounds" include the interplay of perspectives and testimony from former prisoners and victims' families, the political contextualization of the Rebellion, discussions on the implications of mass incarceration, and the highlighting of Rochester leaders, specifically Raymond Scott and Franklin Florence of FIGHT and Elliot "L.D." Barkley, a leader amongst the prisoners. Highlighting the role of grassroots leaders in the Attica Rebellion is part of a growing body of scholarship that prioritizes a top-down approach to analyzing the broader Black Power Movement.[4] *Attica* and "Open Wounds" both provide rich narratives of the play-by-play of the Attica Rebellion, and both offer insight into the dense social and political contexts that fostered the Rebellion. Yet, room remains to address the continued legacy of Attica—namely, mass incarceration and the prison system in New York State. Indeed, "Open Wounds" explicitly acknowledges the impact of the Rockefeller Drug Laws on communities of color.

"Open Wounds: The 50-Year Legacy of the Attica Prison Uprising"

The "Open Wounds" poster exhibit was on view at the Central Library of Rochester & Monroe County from September 2021 through January 2022. The main portion of the traveling exhibit was developed by the New York State Museum. Additional "Local Connections" content for the Rochester installation was curated by Chris Christopher, Gary Craig, and Christine L. Ridarsky. Upon entering the "Open Wounds" exhibit, the visitor is inundated with a flood of red color,

The "Open Wounds: The 50-Year Legacy of the Attica Prison Uprising" poster exhibit on view at the Central Library of Rochester & Monroe County. *Photo courtesy of the Rochester Public Library.*

with bold accents of black and white. The sanguine color scheme forges an obvious, but likely unintended, connection between the display and the content of the exhibit. Yet, there is something much deeper penetrating the erected gray walls and content-rich posters that line the gallery space; a fresh look into the local heroes of the Attica Rebellion. Perhaps the most relevant and groundbreaking fixture of the exhibit is the highlighting of how local leaders like Elliott (L.D.) James Barkley, Raymond Scott, Franklin Florence, and Monroe County Medical Examiner Dr. John Edland played key roles in shaping the Attica Rebellion.

The content is structured both chronologically and thematically. It begins with a close look at local connections and leaders, focusing on L.D. Barkley's leadership and the significance of his role in Attica. At the time of the Rebellion, Barkley was a twenty-one-year old from Rochester who was chosen as a spokesperson for the Attica Brothers. "Open Wounds" captures the humanity and relatability of Barkley—an "impassioned and outspoken" young man, he was revered by his peers for being "extremely intelligent and genuinely personable."[5] In a rare historical moment, Barkley's life is reclaimed as he is remembered for his bravery and leadership during the Rebellion. He was a main orator for the Attica Brothers, a good choice, as his sister remembers him as "an eloquent speaker . . . without

a dangerous bone in his body."[6] Barkley was incarcerated at Attica for a technical parole violation (he did not have a driver's license) for an original charge of cashing a forged money order for $124. His brilliant mind, aspirations, and his vigor for life were brutally suppressed when he was murdered by New York State Police during the retaking of the prison.

Barkley is a particularly tragic but poignant figure in Attica for several reasons. First, his story reflects that of many other young Black men in America. He was captured within a carceral system that overrepresented Black and Hispanic men. Barkley could be anyone's son, brother, or cousin. Whether we fast forward to Trayvon Martin or harken back to lynching victims in the twentieth-century US South, we find endless examples of young Black men entrapped by societal threats of violence, incarceration, and death. Second, his life was plagued by illogical yet omnipresent manifestations of racism and discrimination, a fact evidenced in every geographic, spatial, and intangible dimension of his life. Attica as a prison and a town only mirrored the racialized socioeconomic hierarchy of the larger society. Third, Barkley and his family were from Rochester and were politically active. One of Barkley's sisters, Betty Barkley, was the chair of FIGHT's Prison Reform and Justice Committee. Spotlighting Barkley was a strong move on a multitude of layers for the "Open Wounds" exhibit.

A "Local Connections" poster follows with an overview of the Attica Brothers' manifesto of demands. In sum, prisoners protested against violence, maltreatment, and neglect inflicted upon them by prison staff. The Attica Brothers demanded legal representation, adequate medical treatment, protection of their rights to dissent, and a stipulation that prison laborers be paid standard wages and be permitted to join a labor union. Their demands reflected a broader Black Power precedent. The exhibit quickly transitions into a deeper dive into the Rochester observers, including then-current and former FIGHT presidents Raymond Scott and Minister Franklin Florence. Observers played key roles as negotiators during the

"Open Wounds" exhibit poster. *Photo courtesy of the Rochester Public Library.*

Attica Prison Rebellion; prisoners specifically requested representation from the Black community in Rochester to navigate the complexities of Attica. Perhaps the most heartbreaking takeaway from this component of the exhibit is the reality that most observers believed that a peaceful retaking of the prison was possible; instead, negotiations reached an impasse when Governor Nelson Rockefeller grew impatient, and prisoners refused to sign any agreement unless they were guaranteed immunity. The suspense builds as Rockefeller's unearthed conversation with Richard Nixon is exposed. Rockefeller crudely stated, "You see it's the Black business . . . he had to do it." Moments like this, where the political realities and cruelties that underpinned Attica are revealed, transcend time to move viewers today.

The exhibit then moves onto details of the massacre itself. Here is where more physical artifacts would be helpful in bringing the reality of the Rebellion to life. Unfortunately, the COVID-19 pandemic forced the New York State Museum to scale down its original plan for a more robust traveling exhibit that would have included artifacts from its collection. The Rochester curators supplemented the posters with a single display case containing a jacket that was recovered from the prison and then returned to a local family. The jacket had been worn by a player for the Brown Bombers prison football team. A team member had been punished with solitary confinement after an altercation in the yard the day before the uprising, angering other inmates. Scholars have pointed to the event as a tipping point that caused existing tensions to boil over.

The subsequent poster on Monroe County Medical Examiner John Edland provides a unique perspective into the intricacies and politicization of Attica. Edland rejected Rockefeller's and other authorities' coercions to falsely and publicly claim that prisoners killed hostages by slashing their throats. Instead, Edland concluded that the hostages died by the same bullets as the prisoners: those from New York State Police and National Guard forces. For revealing the truth that hostages were killed by state actors, Edland was subjected to threats from police and civilians that eventually derailed his career and mental health.

The final group of posters follows the

aftermath of the Rebellion. In its attempt to center the perspectives of victims' families, it focuses on the families of hostage victims and fails to dig more deeply into the complexities of race, or to use Attica—a rural, majority-white town sandwiched between two epicenters of deindustrialization, with the prison as the main employer—as a point to analyze broader social issues of race and class during the 1960s. This section also misses an opportunity to focus on how Black communities immediately commemorated the Attica Rebellion as an extension of Black Power in the region, with direct connections to grassroots leaders such as Franklin Florence and Raymond Scott.

In the "Reckonings in Rochester" poster, the state's McKay report is examined, and more local connections are acknowledged; RIT's Director of Development Dorothy Wadsworth is noted as a member of the landmark commission. Here, the exhibit traces the state's response to Attica, detailing several lawsuits from prisoners' and hostage victims' families, state task forces and commissions, and the state's refusal to offer an official apology. The exhibit ends with "Attica is All of Us," a panel that initiates a discussion on the legacy of Attica and how it continues to permeate our society, our consciousness, and especially the lived experiences of Black individuals and communities. A broader discussion of mass incarceration is present here, and some data is provided to contextualize the impact of mass incarceration in the country.

A deeper consideration of women within the context of Attica would have been welcome. The nature of Attica dictates that most of the actors were men. However, we also know that women were greatly impacted by Attica; it had a significant and profound impact on women as mothers, siblings, wives, and daughters of prisoners and hostage victims. Black women in BUILD developed a system to track the injuries and deaths at Attica, and to collect data on the Rebellion and its victims to prepare for future litigation.

Attica

Where "Open Wounds" shines in highlighting the local connections in the Rebellion, *Attica* succeeds in raising national consciousness about the massacre.

It comes as no surprise that Heather Thompson, author of *Blood in the Water: The Attica Prison Uprising of 1971 and Its Legacy,* served as the main historical consultant on the project. The 116-minute documentary flows in a similar chronological order—suspense-building-pinnacle moment—to *Blood in the Water.* The main alteration is the rich addition of interviews with former prisoners, family members of slain hostages, observers, and reporters. These interviews offer a fertile cross-section of analysis from which the complexities of the Attica Rebellion can be slowly untangled. Interviews with Dee Quinn Miller, the daughter of slain correctional officer and Attica's first victim, William Quinn, epitomize the complications and complexities of Attica. Quinn was brutally assaulted by inmates during the taking of the prison; however, he was subsequently brought to medical staff by other inmates. The senseless heartbreak and suffering of Quinn and his family is layered by testimony from former prisoners in the piecing together of the Attica narrative. There is nothing clean or linear about this.

This makes the interviews with Attica prisoners that much more wildly informative and insightful. In fact, the biggest takeaway of *Attica* is how relatable the goal of the Attica Brothers was to all:

freedom, even though it would cost them "in spades."[7] This instinctual fight for freedom often resulted in a contradictory confluence of organization and chaos that comprised the "planning" during the Rebellion. Immediately after the taking of the D-Yard, for example, a flow of natural organization ensued. Prisoners created a system to distribute food. Former Vietnam veterans-turned-inmates set up tents and dug impromptu latrines. Prisoners were assigned roles to uphold the fledgling

Promotional poster for Attica documentary. *Photo courtesy of the Rochester Public Library.*

structure of Rebellion that they had fought hard to achieve. This delicate balance of chaos and order is exemplified by testimony from observers like ABC reporter John Johnson, who recalls his sudden and unwelcomed calling to serve as a prisoner liaison.

These comprehensive interviews from diverse perspectives also open up immensely important and raw conversations about race and class in America that are relevant today. The background and video on Attica as an economic "prison town" arouses a frank discussion about post-war suburbanization, rural America, and the deindustrialization of U.S. cities—particularly in the Rustbelt—during the 1970s. The town's main sources of employment were dairy farms and Attica Correctional Facility. This gives us insight into some of the foundational differences between Attica's correctional officers and prisoners, most of whom were sent to Western New York from New York City. The demographics of the town of Attica—97 percent white in 1970—also feature heavily in the telling of the story.[8] The Black and Hispanic former prisoners interviewed in *Attica* identify this stark racial divide as foundational to the discriminatory and inhumane treatment to which they were subjected; they recall living in two separate spheres of reality. Attica is a point for analysis at the center of those experiences.

Yet more layers emerge to complicate the narrative. The political aspirations of Governor Nelson Rockefeller weighed heavily in the slaughter. Indeed, Clarence Jones argues that Rockefeller's political ambitions obscured his ability to distinguish between hostages and prisoners during the retaking of the prison. Instead, Jones suggests that the decision to retake the prison by force was a calculated move to boost Rockefeller's political law-and-order rhetoric and bid for the vice presidency. Anger still raw in his voice and tears quickly swelling, Jones passionately convinces us that the state was "interested in showing the naked fist of power" under the law-and-order pretext, despite the painfully obvious alternative to peacefully end the negotiations with a settlement.

The photographic and video footage in

Attica, accompanied by direct testimony from victims' families, former prisoners, reporters, and observers, force us to visualize the realities of Attica. The aerial still of Attica Brother and leader Frank Smith, nicknamed "Big Black," depicts an instantly recognizable power dynamic. In the photo, Smith lies naked and restrained in-between two white, armed law enforcement agents. The background story tells us that Smith was tortured for days. The visual is reminiscent of slavery and its underlying power structure. Despite his attempts, Smith had no autonomy over his own body. He was threatened by death if his movements did not accord with the whims of his overseers. This can be extrapolated to the larger systems of power that shadowed over Attica.

A major area of overlap between *Attica* and "Open Wounds" is the focus on Rochester prisoner L.D. Barkley and observer and former FIGHT president Raymond Scott (although *Attica* focuses predominantly on Clarence Jones and John Johnson). The significance of the observers is brought to light through the interviews in the film. James Asbury, a former Attica prisoner, denotes that the observers were critical sounding boards and liaisons; they listened to the Attica Brothers, and made them feel understood and supported. As in "Open Wounds," *Attica* highlights the role of Barkley as a leader and master orator. Interviews with former prisoners reveal that Barkley was still alive after the initial slaughter of inmates. However, he was targeted during the retaking of the prison because of his leadership role. Guardsmen eventually located Barkley, dragged him to the A-Block yard, and executed him.

The retaking of the prison was cold-blooded and brutal. It is critical to recall that prisoners had no firearms. They were exposed to the elements in the D-Yard. Once Rockefeller gave the A-OK to the State Police, National Guardsmen, and local law enforcement groups that had been hovering outside of the prison, they mercilessly fired into the crowd of prisoners and hostages. There was no discernment involved in shooting. State and national forces inflicted gory corporal damage to a range of souls. One prisoner had his eyes shot out by guards, postmortem. Many more were shot in the groin by police in fits of rage.[9] There were more than 400 prisoner injuries reported following the Attica Rebellion; only eight were permitted to leave for medical treatment.[10]

The aftermath of the Rebellion on hostage victims' families was equally brutal. Interviews with the Valone family—whose father Carl Valone was held hostage by inmates and killed by state forces during the retaking of the prison—reveal the penetratingly raw impact of Attica on a spectrum of lives. To this day, the pain of their loss stings just as strong. The numbness and shock is impossible to shake, as the sequence of events that led to the uprising and outcome were simply inexplicable. The victims' families express understandable rage toward the prisoners for causing the uproar and towards the state for not protecting their beloved family members and avoiding legal and financial obligations towards hostage victims' families.

Conclusion

Apart from the official report of the New York State Special Commission on Attica, New York State's public acknowledgment of the horrors of Attica is relatively new. However, the commemoration of the Rebellion in Black communities—especially in Rochester and Buffalo—has been practiced for decades. In Buffalo, BUILD organized a "Black Friday," where Black youth would stay home from school and adults would stay home from work to honor the Attica Brothers. Black communities also organized fundraisers for the legal defense of surviving prisoners. Attica was representative of all past and future police and state-sanctioned violence toward Black communities and, thus, would not be forgotten nor excused.

Attica is moreover poignant because it directly confronts the raw, throbbing issues of today: race, police brutality, and class. At the time of the massacre, 54 percent of Attica's prison population was Black, despite a less than 12 percent Black population in New York State at the time.[11] The state's official report on the Rebellion even acknowledges this: "For the [survivors] . . . memories of a heavy gunfire barrage . . . friends torn open by shotguns and killed by random bullets, beatings . . . and the stark racial hatred and curses by law enforcement officers . . . confirmed for many what they had come to expect from the law."[12] *Attica* and "Open Wounds" expose a paradox about the Attica Rebellion: Although the prisoners were directly challenging the very fabric of American society, their spirit and the essence of the Rebellion were an extension of American ideologies. Clarence Jones, observer and publisher of *The Amsterdam News*, summarizes this contradiction succinctly: "Attica is a symbol of hope. The struggle for self-dignity . . . show us what yet may be possible in the search for meaningful brother and sisterhood in our society."

What comes next in New York State's fraught relationship with incarceration is in flux. Efforts at advancing criminal justice reform legislation, such as Raise the Age and Bail Reform, have resurfaced as highly politicized issues. Addressing those issues today requires us to remember the history that brought us to this present moment. Confronting the horrors of the Attica Prison Rebellion is a crucial and necessary step in a journey to remedy the larger racial injustices that have shaped our state, and our country, in peculiar ways. We must be committed to continuously revisiting the legacy of Attica to avoid its repetition. ■

1. See Leily Arzy and Ram Subramanian, "State Policing Since George Floyd's Murder," *Brennan Center for Justice*, May 21, 2021.
2. Martin Arnold, "Auburn Prisoners Hold 50 Hostages Eight Hours," *New York Times*, November 5, 1970. The hostages included correctional officers and construction workers.
3. New York State Museum, "Rochester Connections," "Open Wounds: The 50-Year Legacy of the Attica Prison Uprising," 2021. The exhibition panels can be downloaded at http://www.nysm.nysed.gov/exhibitions/open-wounds-attica-prison-uprising.
4. See Shanleigh Corrallo, "BUILDing support for the FIGHT: Local Black Power Organizing during the Attica Prison Rebellion of 1971," *Afro Americans in New York Life and History* 42, no. 2 (July 2021).
5. "Open Wounds."
6. Ibid.
7. *Attica*, directed by Traci Curry and Stanley Nelson, released November 2021.
8. U.S. Census Bureau, General Population Characteristics 1970, 26, https://www2.census.gov/library/publications/decennial/1970/pc-v2/15872858v2ch4.pdf.

9. Corrallo, 117.
10. Ibid.
11. New York State Special Commission on Attica, *Attica: The Official Report of the New York State Special Commission on Attica,* (New York: Bantam Books, 1972), 490, and Campbell Gibson and Kay Jung, HISTORICAL CENSUS STATISTICS ON POPULATION TOTALS BY RACE, 1790 TO 1990, AND BY HISPANIC ORIGIN, 1970 TO 1990, FOR THE UNITED STATES, REGIONS, DIVISIONS, AND STATES, September 2002.
12. New York State Special Commission on Attica, 467.